KU-026-426

BHAVNA HAS BEEN WORKING WITH HAIR SINCE GRADUATING FROM LEICESTER SOUTHFIELDS COLLEGE IN 1987.

*A member of City & Guilds, VTCT - Awarding body and Institute for Learning (IfL).*

After working in different salons Bhavna opened her first salon at the age of 21. During this time Bhavna was invited to become an assessor and went on to become a college lecturer at a number of establishments, including Loughborough College, North Warwickshire and Hinckley College and currently New College Nottingham. Since beginning her training, Bhavna has always been at the cutting edge of hair design, winning competitions for her own work and that of her students. She lives in Leicester with her son Ricchi, who has been her motivation to get up every day and achieve her dreams.

Copyright © BHAVNA CHAMPANERI 2010

Copyright © BHAVNA CHAMPANERI 2010

# "NEVER BE AFRAID OF HARD WORK"

I AM PROUD TO WRITE THIS IN CELEBRATION OF THE HARD WORK AND DETERMINATION SHOWN BY BHAVNA CHAMPANERI IN FULFILLING HER LIFELONG DREAM OF WRITING THIS BOOK.

Bhavna has been in the hairdressing industry since 1987 and still shows the passion and love of the industry that first led her into the profession. I have known her personally for 10 years and have witnessed her quiet but focused determination to succeed in whatever she turns her head to, whether it be teaching or actually taking part on a course herself.

Her career has taken her into the world of training and assessing through working as a College Lecturer, which gave her the idea of writing this book to compliment and enrich the training materials of students at the start of their career.

Education and training is key to Bhavna and overcoming any hurdle is a credit to her. She has lived with being dyslexic but still, through her inner determination, has achieved her lifelong dream of writing this book.

Her motto 'NEVER BE AFRAID OF HARD WORK' is a good one for the students who will enjoy and use this book as a resource to further their careers and become the hairdressers of the future.

*William Wilson*
*Head of Technical and*
*Creative Direction*
*Goldwell UK*

*William Wilson*
*Goldwell Creative Director*

# ON TREND

## A Guide on Hair Up Do's

by Bhavna Champaneri

Copyright © BHAVNA CHAMPANERI 2010

Copyright © BHAVNA CHAMPANERI 2010

# CONTENTS

Copyright © BHAVNA CHAMPANERI 2010

# 'Gangster Moll'
## SOFT FINGER WAVE
## AND PIN CURLS

"GANGSTER MOLL harks back to the 1920's and 30's America during prohibition – think of the classic films, 'Some like it Hot' and 'Bugsy Malone'. "

Preparation:

* **Prepare hair a day in advance.**
* **Pre-colour Hair with a Demi/Quasi Permanent colour.**
* **Shampoo and Condition Hair.**
* **Apply a Styling Lotion to damp hair and blow dry using a flat brush.**

* Section off the front panel *(approximately 6-7cm)*.
* Clip section out of the way.
* Brick wind the remaining hair using medium size heated rollers.
* When the rollers have cooled remove, *(after approximately 20 minutes)*,
* Use a flat brush to form a ponytail to one side, securing with a band.
* From tip to point, wind the hair *(anti-clockwise)* into pin curls and secure with hair grips.
* Continue with the remaining hair until you have formed the shape of a bun.

Front section:

* Apply a Volumising Gel and form into a soft finger wave moulding wet hair into "S" shape movements using hands, fingers and a comb.
* Take the tail end of the hair and incorporate into a bun.
* Secure with hair grips.

Copyright © BHAVNA CHAMPANERI 2010

**MAC Make-Up**

| | |
|---|---|
| **Base** | MAC Scrobe Cream |
| **Foundation** | MAC Studio Sculpt Foundation |
| **Concealer** | MAC Studio Sculpt Concealer |
| **Powder** | MAC Mineralize Natural Powder 'Medium' |
| **Blusher** | MAC 'Peachykeen' |
| **Eye shadow** | MAC 'All That Glitters' on the lid, 'Bronze' on the crease |
| **Highlighter** | MAC 'Nylon' |
| **Eye brow** | MAC 'Spiked' |
| **Eyeliner** | MAC 'Fascinating' on waterline. 'Boot Black' on the lid |
| **Mascara** | MAC Prolong lash 'Pitch Black' |
| **False eye lashes** | MAC #30 |
| **Lip liner** | MAC 'Dervish' |
| **Lipstick** | MAC 'Shy Girl' |
| **Lip gloss** | MAC Dazzle Glass 'Internationalist' |

Copyright © BHAVNA CHAMPANERI 2010

A Guide To Hair Up Do's

Copyright © BHAVNA CHAMPANERI 2010

A Guide To Hair Up Do's

# 'Roll out the Barrel'
## BARREL CURLS

Preparation:

- **Prepare hair a day in advance.**
- **Pre-colour Hair with a Highlift Blonde.**
- **Shampoo and Condition Hair.**
- **Apply a blow-dry lotion to damp hair and blow dry using a large round brush.**

- Section the hair from the crown to behind the ears on both sides.
- Slick the back section into a ponytail above the occipital bone using a pea sized amount of Spray Wax.
- Secure with a band.
- Starting just above the ponytail, take a 2.5cm wide section of hair, wind the hair from the tip to the root using your two index fingers to form a 'barrel'.
- Secure using grips, ensuring they sit against the scalp under the 'barrel'.
- Continue this process with the remaining hair arranging the 'barrel curls' to form a bun.

Front section:

- Starting from the base, divide the hair into approximately 5cm sections.
- Take each section and, using heated irons, create soft waves by moving the iron 90 degrees forward and back as you slowly move down the hair.
- Part the hair on one side.
- Sweep the large section around and incorporate into the 'barrel curl bun'.
- Fix securely with grips.
- Take the remaining section and slick back firmly to the head. Again, incorporate into the bun.
- Finish with Shine Spray.

**MAC Make-Up**

| | |
|---|---|
| **Base** | MAC 'Prep and Prime Face skin base' |
| **Foundation** | MAC 'Select SPF 15 Foundation' |
| **Concealer** | MAC Studio Sculpt Concealer |
| **Blusher** | MAC 'Danity' |
| **Eye shadow** | MAC 'Electra 'on inner corner, 'Vex' all over the lid, 'Carbon' and 'Scene' on the crease |
| **Eye brow** | MAC 'Lingering' |
| **Eyeliner** | MAC 'Pointblack' |
| **Mascara** | MAC 'Prolash' black |
| **Lip liner** | MAC 'Cherry' |
| **Lipstick** | MAC 'Russian Red' |

Copyright © BHAVNA CHAMPANERI 2010

# 'Rapunzel'
## LETTING YOUR HAIR DOWN!

'ROLLOUT THE BARREL' can be transformed into 'Rapunzel' by:

• Removing all the hair grips and brushing the hair to one side.

• Dress the curls out with Shine Spray which creates definition.

• Take the fringe and straighten out the previous soft waves.

• Sweep this around and incorporate it behind the ears.

• Finish with a light Hairspray.

## MAC Make-Up

| | |
|---|---|
| **Base** | MAC Studio Moisture Fix |
| **Foundation** | MAC Studio Fix Fluid |
| **Blusher** | MAC 'Plum Foolery' |
| **Concealer** | MAC Studio Finish Concealer |
| **Eye shadow** | MAC 'Bitter' on lid, 'Swimming' and 'Carbon' on crease |
| **Highlighter** | MAC Cremebase 'Pearl' |
| **Eye brow** | MAC 'Phloof' |
| **Eyeliner** | MAC 'Black Boot' |
| **Mascara** | MAC Pro Lash 'Coal Black' |
| **False eye lashes** | MAC #41 |
| **Lip liner** | MAC 'Soar' |
| **Lipstick** | MAC 'Up the amp' |
| **Lip gloss** | MAC 'Clear' |

Copyright © BHAVNA CHAMPANERI 2010

Copyright © BHAVNA CHAMPANERI 2010

# 'Extensions'
## A HAIR WEFT

A way of adding hair to your hair for length, volume, colour, high lights etc. There are different ways of adding extensions and one of them is the Track Weave.

"WIGS WERE VERY EXPENSIVE. Those who could not afford to buy wigs used hair extensions. These were preferred as they could be tied up. Thicker hair was considered as ideal by the Eygyptians, so they attached hair extensions to their wigs to enhance their appearance."

**Track weave:** Using human hair wefts to create a track of extensions. Tracking is a much safer method of adding extensions to the human hair by weaving. The wefts hair is a bunch of hair sewn across a ribbon.

The weft hair is added on a track of cornrows. Wefts are made in two ways: machine and hand-made. When wefts are handmade they can provide quite a natural look.

The benefit of wefts on tracks is that they can actually be stitched into your hair and do not require any chemicals which would normally damage your hair.

**Tracking: adding hair on a cornrow track:**

Preparation:

• **Wash and condition hair.**

• **Blow dry with a Styling Lotion.**

• **Select a hair weft that closely matches your natural hair.**

• Section a thin line of your hair from temple to temple about 0.5cm wide. *Remember not to be too close to the hair line so as to give a more natural look as well as to take away discomfort.*

• Braid a cornrow from one temple to the middle of the head (*approximately 5cm above the occipital bone for a ponytail style*) and secure with a band.

• Braid another cornrow from the other side of the temple and meet at the point the previous cornrow stopped.

• Secure in the centre of the back of the head (*approximately 5cm above the occipital bone*).

• Secure both strands with bands.

• Further cornrows can be added in similar design as the first one. Check the head to decide how much cornrows you want to add. Usually between 3 to 5 tracks are used for a full head of design.

• For the stitching, use a curved needle with a nylon sewing thread that closely matches the hair colour.

• Over stitch the hair weft on to the cornrow. *Nylon thread will be strong enough to be washed and styled.*

• Style as required.

*It is strongly recommended that hair extensions are put in and maintained by a trained and skilled salon.*

*Extensions will last for approximately 4-6 weeks.*

Copyright © BHAVNA CHAMPANERI 2010

Forward plait

Copyright © BHAVNA CHAMPANERI 2010

# 'Like Bees to Honey'
## Classic Bee Hive

### Preparation:
Model 1

- **Pre-colour Hair with a Demi/Quasi Permanent colour.**
- **Shampoo and Condition Hair.**
- **Apply Blow-Dry Lotion to damp hair and blow dry using a flat brush.**

THE 'BEE HIVE' is believed to have originated in America in 1958 and was highly popular throughout the 60s. Worn by Audrey Hepburn's character, Holly Golightly, in the classic film 'Breakfast at Tiffanys,' it is a style that endures. This style can be worn for day and evening; look for accessories to customise your own version.

### Model 1

- First, section off the fringe.
- Section the hair above the ears *(above the occipital bone)*.
- Work with the top section to backcomb the hair.
  *Do this by working from the base up, using small sections until you have created volume.*
- Take the fringe, gently backcomb and incorporate into beehive.
- Using a flat brush, smooth the outer layer of the hair to form a bee hive.
- Secure with grips.
- Finish with a light Hairspray.

Copyright © BHAVNA CHAMPANERI 2010

## Preparation

- **Pre-colour Hair with a Pre-Lightener.**
- **Shampoo and Condition Hair.**
- **Apply a Blow-dry lotion to damp hair and blow dry using a flat brush.**

- First, section off the fringe.
- Section the hair above the ears *(above the occipital bone).*
- Work with the top section to backcomb the hair. *Do this by working from the base up, using small sections until you have created volume.*
- Using a flat brush, smooth the outer layer of the hair to form a bee hive.
- Secure with grips.
- Sweep the fringe across and blend into the beehive.
- Finish with a light Hairspray.

## MAC Make-Up

| | |
|---|---|
| **Base** | MAC Scrobe cream |
| **Foundation** | MAC Studio Fix Foundation |
| **Concealer** | MAC Studio Finish Concealer |
| **Powder** | MAC Mineralize powder |
| **Blusher** | MAC 'Pink Swoon' |
| **Eye shadow** | MAC 'Vex' on lid, 'Print' on crease |
| **Highlighter** | MAC Crème Base 'Pearl' |
| **Eye brow** | MAC 'Lingering' |
| **Eyeliner** | MAC 'Black Boot' |
| **Mascara** | MAC X-Thicker 'Black X' |
| **False eye lashes** | MAC #12 |
| **Lipstick** | MAC 'Chatterbox' |

Copyright © BHAVNA CHAMPANERI 2010

# 'Pre-Raphaelite'
## PLAITS AND CURLS

CASCADING, RED TRESSES OF HAIR were synonymous with the models featured in the paintings of the scandalous and controversial Pre-Raphaelite brotherhood, and in particular, the work of Dante Gabriel Rossetti to create erotic overtones in these romantic, yet escapist, works of art.

Preparation:

- **Pre-colour hair with a Demi/Quasi Permanent.**
- **Shampoo and Condition hair.**
- **Apply a Heat Protection Styling Lotion to damp hair and blow dry using a flat brush.**

- Section the hair starting from a side parting, around and above the ear down to the side of the neck. This should be approximately 7.5cm wide.
- Use a 3 strand Scalp Plait to work the hair from the parting to the nape.
- Secure with a band and grips.
- Work from the opposite side of the parting, taking a 7.5cm section to the ear.
- Again, create a 3 strand Scalp Plait finishing behind the ear.
- Secure with a grip.
- To create body at the crown, gently tease the hair to create height.
- Sweep the loose hair around to one side and secure it with a band.
- Starting at the nape of the neck and working with small sections (*approximately an 2.5cm*), use a curling iron to form loose curls with the remaining hair.
- Continue until you have curled all of the hair.
- Secure individual and naturally falling curls with grips to form a loose bun.
- Work Soft Wax into the curls to sculpt and add definition.
- Finish with a light Hairspray.

Copyright © BHAVNA CHAMPANERI 2010

**MAC Make-Up**

| | |
|---|---|
| **Base** | MAC Prime and Prep Skin |
| **Foundation** | MAC Studio Fix Studio |
| **Concealer** | MAC Select Cover-Up |
| **Powder** | MAC Prep and Prime Transparent Finishing Powder |
| **Blusher** | MAC Bronzing Powder "Golden" |
| **Eye shadow** | MAC 'Carbon' and 'Typographic', 'Blacktrack' for lace |
| **Eye brow** | MAC 'Spiked' |
| **Mascara** | MAC Pro Lash 'Coal Black' |
| **False eye lashes** | MAC #3 and #7 |
| **Lipstick** | MAC 'Hang up' |

Copyright © BHAVNA CHAMPANERI 2010

A Guide To Hair Up Do's

# 'Studio 54'
## CRIMPING

THE MODERN CRIMPING IRON WAS INVENTED BY GERI CUSENZA IN 1972. Crimped hair was widely seen in the late 70's and 80's and during the heady disco days of New York's Famous Studio 54. This modern take on those decades creates a style that embodies the best of that era with a classic shape.

Preparation:

- **Prepare the hair a day in advance or on the day.**
- **Pre-colour hair with a Highlift Blonde.**
- **Shampoo and Condition hair.**
- **Apply Heat Protection Styling Lotion to damp hair and blow dry with a flat brush.**

- Section the hair from the nape of the neck.
- Use crimping irons to work from the root of the hair to the tip.
- Continue until the whole head of hair has been crimped.
- Sweep the hair back into a ponytail (*moderate tension*).
- Securing with a band just below the occipital bone.
- Divide the ponytail into 2.
- Take each section and working with the tail end, loosely wrap the hair into 2 large barrel curl.
- Secure with grips at the nape.
- Gently 'tease' the 2 barrels to form a horizontal chignon.
- Finish with Strong Styling Lotion.

Copyright © BHAVNA CHAMPANERI 2010

Copyright © BHAVNA CHAMPANERI 2010

# 'Future 40's'
## soft curls

THE SOLUTION FOR MOST 1940S women in wartime Britain and America was short layered hairstyles which could be curled, rolled and waved. This style combines the glamour of this time with modern accessories.

Preparation:

- **Pre-colour hair with a Demi/Quasi Permanent colour.**
- **Shampoo and Condition hair.**
- **Apply Heat Protection Styling Lotion to damp hair and blow dry using a flat brush.**

- Section the hair from the crown to the forehead (*approximately 15cm square*).
- Divide this into 3 rows from the crown to the forehead.
- Take each row and direction wind 3 heated rollers from point to root to base.
- When cool, gently remove the rollers.
- Use a flat brush to dress out and form 3 large 'barrel rolls' from alternate directions.
- Secure with grips.
- Apply an accessory clip if desired.
- Finish with a light Hairspray.

### MAC Make-Up

| | |
|---|---|
| **Base** | MAC Fix + |
| **Foundation** | MAC Studio Moisture Tint SPF 15 |
| **Blusher** | MAC 'Ladybrush' |
| **Eye shadow** | MAC 'Blanc Type' |
| **Eye brow** | MAC 'Fling' |
| **Mascara** | MAC Splashproof Lash 'Blacksplash' |
| **Lip** | MAC Lip Conditioner Stick |

Copyright © BHAVNA CHAMPANERI 2010

Copyright © BHAVNA CHAMPANERI 2010

Learning Resource Centre

# 'Rock Vision'
## barrel rolls and twist plait

Preparation:

- **Pre-colour hair with Pre-Lightener and tone with a Demi/Quasi Permanent colour.**
- **Shampoo and Condition hair.**
- **Apply mousse to damp hair and blow dry using a flat brush.**

- Divide the front hair approximately above the mid eyebrow to give a middle and 2 sides.
- Take one side section and divide into 3 horizontal sections.
- Scalp Plait each section to just past the ears and secure with hair grips.
- Take the other side section and again, divide into 3 horizontal sections.
- Twist each section tightly to the scalp just behind the ears and secure with grips.
- Form the middle section into 3 large barrel curls and secure with grips.
- Tease and backcomb the remaining hair to create volume and texture.
- Apply a small amount of Spray Wax to the ends to create definition.
- Finish with Shine Spray.

Copyright © BHAVNA CHAMPANERI 2010

**MAC Make-Up**

| | | |
|---|---|---|
| **Base** | MAC | Studio Moisture Fix SPF 15 |
| **Foundation** | MAC | Mineralize Foundation SPF 15 |
| **Concealer** | MAC | Studio Sculpt Concealer |
| **Powder** | MAC | Prep & Prime Finishing Powder |
| **Blusher** | MAC | 'Dollymix' |
| **Eye shadow** | MAC | 'Blacktrack' and 'Carbon'. (Extra black glittery) |
| **Highlighter** | MAC | Iridescent Loose Powder 'Sliver Dusk' |
| **Eye brow** | MAC | 'Velvetone' |
| **Eyeliner** | MAC | 'Smolder' |
| **Mascara** | MAC | Zoom Fast Black Lash |
| **False eye lashes** | MAC | #7 and #36 |
| **Lip liner** | MAC | 'Stone' |
| **Lip gloss** | MAC | Dazzleglass 'She-dam |

Copyright © BHAVNA CHAMPANERI 2010

Copyright © BHAVNA CHAMPANERI 2010

Copyright © BHAVNA CHAMPANERI 2010

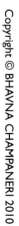
Copyright © BHAVNA CHAMPANERI 2010

# 'Summer Cool'
## ponytail with a wave

**Preparation:**

- **Prepare hair a day in advance.**
- **Pre-colour hair with Highlift Blondes and Lowlights.**
- **Shampoo and Condition Hair.**
- **Apply Heat Protection Styling Lotion to damp hair and blow dry with a flat brush.**

- Take a square section from the front to the crown of the head.
- Secure out of the way with a clip.
- Scrape the remaining hair into a low ponytail.
- Take the square section and divide vertical into 3.
- Taking each section, wrap the hair (*from the root to the tip*) around a curling wand.
- When the 3 strands have been curled, bring them together and using a tail comb, tease the hair upwards to form 2 distinct 'waves'.
- Twist the hair underneath the wave and pin it in to secure the ends.
- Finish with Shine Spray for brilliant shine.

Copyright © BHAVNA CHAMPANERI 2010

# 'Revolution'
## Multiple Loops

Preparation:

- **Prepare hair a day in advance.**
- **Pre-colour hair with Highlift Blondes.**
- **Shampoo and Condition hair.**
- **Apply Blow-dry Lotion to damp hair and blow dry using a large round brush.**

*This style works best with longer hair.*

- Divide the hair into 2 sections, in front of the ears to form an 'extended fringe'.
- Take the back section into a ponytail securing with a band just above the occipital bone.
- Take the front section and create loops across the head, securing with grips.

**Creating a loop:**

- Select approximately 1cm width strand of hair.
- Create the first loop with your thumb and forefinger (*the size can vary depending on the length of the hair*). This can be close or away from the scalp.
- Pull the remaining hair strand through the loop to create another loop.
- Repeat this process until the entire hair strand has been looped.
- Secure the end with a fine grip.
- For the back of the head use a light padding, moulded into the desired shape and secured with grips.
- Finish with a light Hairspray.

Copyright © BHAVNA CHAMPANERI 2010

Copyright © BHAVNA CHAMPANERI 2010

Copyright © BHAVNA CHAMPANERI 2010

## MAC Make-Up

| | | |
|---|---|---|
| **Base** | MAC | Prep & Prime Skin |
| **Foundation** | MAC | Studio Fix Fluid |
| **Concealer** | MAC | Studio Finish Concealer |
| **Powder** | MAC | Mineralize Powder |
| **Blusher** | MAC | Mineralize Powder 'Med Dark' and 'Dark' |
| **Eye shadow** | MAC | 'Steamy' and 'Plumage'. (Extra gold leaves} |
| **Highlighter** | MAC | 'Sliver Dusk' |
| **Eye brow** | MAC | 'Stud' |
| **Eyeliner** | MAC | 'Smolder' |
| **Mascara** | MAC | Pro Lash 'Coal Black' |
| **False eye lashes** | MAC | #7 |
| **Lip liner** | MAC | 'Cushy' |
| **Lip gloss** | MAC | 'Clear' |

Copyright © BHAVNA CHAMPANERI 2010

# 'Twisted Sister'
## Variation on a Twist

**Preparation:**

- **Pre-colour hair with Highlift Blondes.**
- **Shampoo and Condition hair.**
- **Apply Volumising Gel to damp hair.**

*This style requires the hair to be damp when working with it so it is useful to keep a water spray to hand.*

- Part the hair as desired.
- Section the hair horizontally from the crown to the back of each ear.
- Form a low ponytail.
- Working with the front section, twist the hair directional from the front of the head to the back (*from root to point*).
- Take to the back of the head and incorporate with the poinytail.
- Take the ponytail from the nape and twist from root to point until the hair starts to form a coil.
- Tuck the ends in and secure with a hair grip to form a twisted chignon.
- Repeat on the opposite side.
- Finish with a light Hairspray.

*Consider the shape of the face and the person's features as this style does not add height or width.*

Copyright © BHAVNA CHAMPANERI 2010

A Guide To Hair Up Do's

Copyright © BHAVNA CHAMPANERI 2010

# 'Lets Twist Again'
## More Variation on a Twist

• Section the hair as seen in the picture.

• Place the parting where desired.

• Starting at the roots, the hair is turned in the same direction down to the
  points of the hair until the desired twist is achieved. (*It is important to twist
  the hair directional from the front of the head to the back*).

• Bring each twist to the nape of the neck and secure with hair-grips.

• When all the twists are in place gather the remaining hair together
  and twist this until the hair starts to curl and coil itself and form a chignon.

• Secure with hair grips.

• Finish with a light Hairspray.

*Tip: Consider the shape of the face and the person's features as this style does not
     add height or width.*

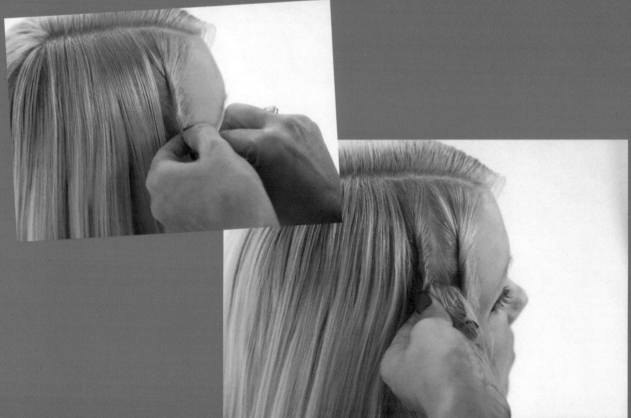

Copyright © BHAVNA CHAMPANERI 2010

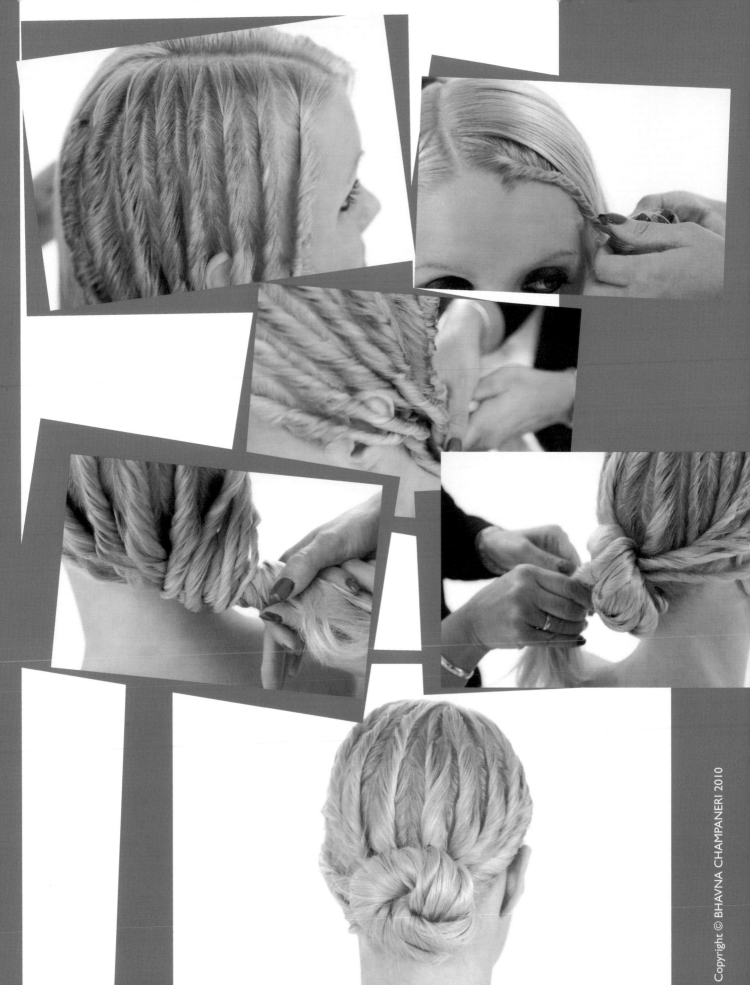

Copyright © BHAVNA CHAMPANERI 2010

# 'Champagne Supernova'
## Creating an impact

*"Lady Gaga this one is for you"*

This design incorporates and recycled objects
to help sculpt and give volume.

- This was inspired by wedding themes.
- You can create your own ideas from your inspirations.
- Models own hair (*no added hair pieces*).

MAC Make-Up

| | |
|---|---|
| **Base** | MAC Fix + |
| **Foundation** | MAC Studio Tech |
| **Powder** | MAC Mineralize powder |
| **Concealer** | MAC Studio Sculpt Concealer |
| **Blusher** | MAC 'Fleur Power' |
| **Eye shadow** | MAC 'Carbon' and Pigment 'Violet' |
| **Eye brow** | MAC 'Stud' |
| **Eyeliner** | MAC 'Smolder' |
| **Mascara** | MAC Dazzle Lash 'Black Dazzle' |
| **False eye lashes** | MAC #36 |
| **Lip liner** | MAC 'Devish' |
| **Lip gloss** | MAC 'Pink Lemonade' |

Copyright © BHAVNA CHAMPANERI 2010

Copyright © BHAVNA CHAMPANERI 2010

# Tips...

1. Remember, as a stylist your appearance is crucial. Set a good example and inspire confidence in your clients by wearing a suitable hairstyle that reflects current fashion.

2. It is important to look at the face shape before deciding on a style - comb the hair back and look at the hair line and face shape before beginning any style.

3. Hair colour: if you are pale skinned, softer tones can be more flattering - too dark or too light can wash out the skin tone.

4. Co-ordinate your hair with your outfit by adding a carefully chosen accessory. It is a cheap and simple way to update your style.

5. It is a fact - your hair grows 1.25 cm a month (on average) so keeping it trimmed every 6-8 weeks keeps your hair looking healthy. It is not just a myth to make hairdressers wealthy!

6. Keep your hair healthy. This is especially important if you are using chemical treatments and heat processes. Use a deep penetrating conditioner once a month.

7. When choosing hair appliances choose carefully. Certain brands and styles give you more scope. For example, certain brands of straighteners allow you to smooth, curl and even crimp the hair!

8. Heat styling: use a good thermal protecting spray to prevent the hair from drying out so when using heated stylers, the tools will take the moisture from the protector and not your hair!

9. Fashion is important but you need to find a style that suits you. Confidence in what you are wearing is essential.

10. When buying hair accessories, for example hair combs, ensure they suit the size of shape of the head. Big can make a statement, too big can look ridiculous!

Copyright © BHAVNA CHAMPANERI 2010

# Tips for Brides...

**1** I would recommend the hair be washed the night before.

**2** Use a light conditioner but avoid serums (*do not saturate the hair as this may make it harder to work with*).

**3** In addition, apply face and body creams carefully, avoiding the hairline.

**4** Apply mousse to damp hair and dry. This will be fabulous for working with the next day!

**5** Start treating your hair to conditioning treatments several weeks before your big day, especially if it is chemically treated, to ensure your stylist does not have to hide damaged hair.

**6** Colours should be retouched the week before the wedding.

**7** When using straighteners, there are 3 sizes:
**Mini** - ideal for short hair, great for root movement and style fringes.
**Styler** – straightens hair, curls hair, create waves ideal for all types of hair.
**Salon styler** - ideal for hair that is thick or really curly to give that slick, straight look.

**8** Pony tails are not just for bad hair days. They can be worn high or low and can look chic and sophisticated.

**9** Consult your stylist before buying a tiara - the shape of your face and hair style must be complemented by the tiara you choose.

**10** Have a trial run with your stylist prior to the wedding to ensure you are happy with your chosen style. You should be planning your hair and make-up approximately 6 months in advance.

**11** Hats and fascinators can either be fantastic accessories or something you regret when you see the wedding photographs! There are several factors to consider before you spend your money: make sure the accessory fits the size of your head and face shape and take a reliable friend who will be honest with you. Consider how you wish your hair to look and talk to your stylist before you buy, as the style you want may not be possible with the accessories you choose.

"**I cannot express how important it is to keep you (and your team) updated with current trends, techniques and products. It keeps you fresh with ideas and enthusiasm.**

**Motivation: it is vital that you and your team feel motivated. Team building is essential to a good working atmosphere. In turn, this will also help build customer loyalty and a business that continues to grow.**"

Copyright © BHAVNA CHAMPANERI 2010

A Guide To Hair Up Do's

# Inspiration & Motivation

So many aspects of my life have inspired me and made me the person I am today. Being dyslexic has driven me to achieve my goals and made me determined to overcome any setbacks. My biggest frustration has been difficulty in expressing my creativity in writing but this book ticks that goal!

*Motivation* - My lifelong fashion guru friend "Sang" and I have always bounced ideas off each other - she is always ahead of the game! Being a good hair designer equals understanding fashion. If you don't, you will be a fashion follower instead of a leader.

*Experimenting* - I am always trying out different techniques and approaches and playing around with what hair can do! Fashion is essential but it is vital to analyse someone's face, hair and personality to create the right look for them.

*Travel* -New York and London remain the epicentres of fashion and design. I love to visit these two cities and gain inspiration from the shows, the architecture, culture and everyday people.

*Youth* - I am lucky to work with the 16-19 years age group who keep me on your toes! Teaching the students hair skills and the skill to keep learning in life generates endless, boundless energy.

Copyright © BHAVNA CHAMPANERI 2010

Copyright © BHAVNA CHAMPANERI 2010

# Thank you...

### My Motto

Never be afraid of hard work. Sometimes this means working around the clock to achieve the goals and dreams in life. *Go for it!*

On Trend emerged from my experiences in the hairdressing industry, working as a salon owner, lecturer and bridal stylist.

History inspires new ideas, building on skills from the past to create new styles and techniques for the future.

"NEVER
BE
AFRAID
OF
HARD
WORK"

## All my thanks go to the following...

Goldwell
Mac Cosmetics UK
Monsoon Accessorize
Dyslexia Action
Denman
Prestige Colour Solutions Limited

### Models

Priya Champaneri
Katrin Kupar
Marie Hilliar
Catrine Hilliar
Milly Moss
Sonia Neale
Kellie Moody

Carla Power - for her brilliant support throughout our photo shoot
Joy Phido
Venture Photography
Prakash Rathod Creative Director
Rebecca Dawe Photography
Sarah Jayne - Jewellery and Tiaras
Darshana Champaneri - Designer and illustrator
Jems Photography

Copyright © BHAVNA CHAMPANERI 2010

Photography courtesy of Ross Underwood @Venture Portraits, Leicester
Ross started his career in Photography at college in 2000. Since then he has gone on to apply his skills to numerous visual mediums including graphic design, digital painting and film production.

Sue Clegg is Head of Art and Design at a Leicestershire school and a practicing artist/designer.

*"I am Bhavna's neighbour and most of the writing of this book took place over many late nights, cups of coffee and the odd glass of wine. Most of all we have had a really good time writing this book!"*

Kellie Moody, 25 and a Make-Up Artist working part time for MAC, lives in Leicester and is profoundly deaf, hearing nothing without hearing aids.

*"I love being a make-up artist, I am a very creative person and love colour and experimenting with new things. I have always loved art and been very artistic, I also love fashion! I am an individual and like to mix new and old together.*

*I had a lot of fun working with Bhavna. I think her work is amazing and unique and I look forward to working with her again in future."*

Copyright © BHAVNA CHAMPANERI 2010

# What people say about Bav:

" Bav has been a very good friend of mine for a number of years. She is incredibly talented and passionate about her work and you will see evidence of this in her new book. She has a very friendly, lively and bubbly personality which is very infectious and makes learning from her a fun experience for her students as well as an informative one. Bav works incredibly hard and deserves every success as she makes things happen! Good luck with your book Hun! "
C x

" Bhavna is a wonderfully talented hairdresser who I have known over 30 years. She is friendly, funny, vivacious, focused, trustworthy, stylish and most important, an amazing friend. She is a fighter, full of determination, drive and ambition. I marvel at what she can get done in a day and this is because she is energetic and passionate about what she does. I would recommend Bav; she is warm hearted and one of the kindest people you could ever hope to meet. "
Jay. x

" Bav, as she is known to her dear friends, is one of those people who always make a positive impression on the people she meets. She has a zest for life and a happy personality that matches her positive outlook. A hard worker and true professional in the "old school" way, Bav is an honest and caring person. These traits come through to her professional life and to top it all she is a great hairdresser!! "
Sang. x

" B's creativity and imagination has always made her stand out in the crowd and become the success story she is today. Her ambition and determination keeps her thriving and constantly reaching for new and exciting heights, both professionally and personally. As a sister she's a lot of fun to be with, always turning a dull moment into a crazy one! She's an inspiration and I know she will continue to inspire me. I wish u all the best with the book and the future. "
Priya. x

Copyright © BHAVNA CHAMPANERI 2010

Copyright © BHAVNA CHAMPANERI 2010

CPSIA information can be obtained
at www.ICGtesting.com
228651LV00006B

Learning Resource Centre